AR Level 7.8

AR Points 1.0

Lexile _____

56

332
.11
APE

GAYLORD M

The Progressive Movement 1900–1920
Efforts to Reform America's New Industrial Society ™

THE FEDERAL RESERVE ACT

Making the American Banking System Stronger

Melanie Ann Apel

rosen central
Primary Source ™

The Rosen Publishing Group, Inc., New York

Published in 2006 by The Rosen Publishing Group, Inc.
29 East 21st Street, New York, NY 10010

Library of Congress Cataloging-in-Publication Data

Apel, Melanie Ann.
The Federal Reserve Act: making the American banking system stronger/by Melanie Ann Apel.
   p. cm.—(The Progressive movement 1900–1920: efforts to reform America's new industrial society)
Includes bibliographical references and index.
ISBN 1-4042-0196-3 (lib. bdg.)
ISBN 1-4042-0863-1 (pbk. bdg.)
6-pack ISBN 1-4042-6186-9
1. Board of Governors of the Federal Reserve System (U.S.)—History—Juvenile literature.
2. Banks and banking—United States—History—20th century—Juvenile literature.
3. Progressivism (United States politics)—Juvenile literature.
I. Title. II. Series.
HG2563.A78 2004
332.1'1'097309041—dc22

                                                2004000749

Manufactured in the United States of America

On the cover: Top: The Federal Reserve Board, circa 1918–1920. Bottom: The Northwest National Bank, Minnesota, circa 1890.

Photo credits: Cover (top), pp. 5, 9, 13 Library of Congress Prints and Photographs Division; cover (bottom) pp. 7, 12 Minnesota Historical Society; p. 10 Getty Images; p. 15 © Underwood & Underwood/Corbis; p. 17 © Hulton-Deutsch Collection/Corbis; pp. 19, 20, 25 © Bettmann/Corbis; p. 21 National Archives; p. 23 Federal Reserve Photo; p. 26 Federal Reserve Bank of New York.

Designer: Les Kanturek; Editor: Mark Beyer; Photo Researcher: Amy Feinberg

Contents

Chapter One

The Progressive Movement

As the nineteenth century was heading into its final decade, a new movement began to take shape in America. It was called the Progressive movement. It lasted from about 1900 to 1920. The Progressive movement made many social and economic programs very popular. Each was meant to make life easier and fairer for the working people of America. The people who worked toward making the changes were called Progressives. They were a group of mostly middle-class American Protestants and immigrant Jews and Catholics.

Progressives were journalists, politicians, and single-cause crusaders who wanted to see progress. Some of these people remained Progressives all their lives. Others faded into the woodwork, forgotten with the end of the era. Nevertheless, this was one time in American history during which ordinary people did extraordinary

VOL. LXVII. No. 1718.   PUCK BUILDING, New York, February 2nd, 1910.   PRICE TEN CENTS.

PUCK

BILLION DOLLAR BANK MERGER

FRANK A.NANKIVELL

THE CENTRAL BANK.

WHY SHOULD UNCLE SAM ESTABLISH ONE, WHEN UNCLE PIERPONT IS ALREADY ON THE JOB?

Financiers owned so many banks that big business had more control over the nation's money supply than the government did. The Progressives, however, wanted the government to be in control. This cartoon from *Puck* shows businessman J. P. Morgan holding New York City banks in his arms.

things. It was highly unusual for so many nonpolitical people to achieve such great progress.

Before the Progressive movement, rich businessmen controlled all the money in the United States. People did not like this. They wanted a new system. They believed that their money should be controlled by the government. Of course, the businessmen were not happy with this. Things were about to change.

Newspaper reporters and writers were investigating everything from labor laws to politics. They wanted to make public the bad things that went on behind closed doors. It was easy for them to get the word out because of something new in publishing. This was called the magazine. Magazines were popular and not very expensive. Many people bought them. Magazines such as *Ladies' Home Journal*, the *Saturday Evening Post*, and *McClure's* published stories of widespread corruption.

People who worked in politics hoped to make important reforms on local, state, and national levels. Some of these key figures were Cleveland mayor Tom Johnson, Wisconsin governor Robert La Follette, and California governor and United States senator Hiram Johnson. Together, these politicians fought against the corruption.

Local governments changed local laws to improve people's everyday lives. This town board in Lakeland, Minnesota, includes local citizens active in the health of their community.

They worked to change the laws that governed voting. They worked on improvements to the working conditions of children and women. They secured plans for insurance for people who got hurt while working. They also created a program of welfare assistance for widows.

Because of the efforts of the Progressives, many changes took place during the time known as the Progressive Era. For example, women's suffrage allowed women the right to vote for government officials and to be elected into government positions. Along with this change in voting came the now-popular voting practices known as initiative, referendum, and recall.

Another change was the National Prohibition Act (also called the Volstead Act because it was written by Andrew J. Volstead), which described "intoxicating liquor as anything having an alcoholic content of anything more than 0.5 percent, omitting alcohol used for medicinal and sacramental purposes." This act was intended to cut down on the amount of alcohol people were drinking in hopes of lowering crime, poverty, and death rates and improving the country's economy and the quality of life for the American people.

The Progressive movement also provided the American labor force with shorter, more manageable work hours. It cut out child labor completely. Thanks to child labor laws, children were no longer required, expected, or even allowed to work full days alongside adults. Still in effect today, child labor laws allow children to work only a certain number of hours per day, depending on the state in

The Progressive movement grew into a national campaign to give more governing power to the people. This photo shows the National Progressive Convention in 1912. It was held in Chicago, Illinois, to decide which candidate should be chosen to appear on the presidential ballot.

which they live, their age, and the type of work they are doing. Social welfare programs were put into place to give government financial assistance to low-income families. Income tax payment requirements were changed to match a family's or an individual's income.

The Progressive Party was also known as the Bull Moose Party. The party only lasted about sixteen years, but it created many positive changes for American citizens.

Most of these new programs were part of the principles and policies called the Progressive Party platform of 1912. The Progressive Party, which lasted until 1916, was also known as the Bull Moose Party. Theodore Roosevelt ran this party. He also served as president of the United States from 1901 until 1909.

There was one more important change that took place during the Progressive movement—the adoption of the new Federal Reserve Act. The Federal Reserve Act, which was put into place on December 23, 1913, was "an act to provide for the establishment of Federal reserve banks, to furnish an elastic currency, to afford means of rediscounting commercial paper, to establish a more effective supervision of banking in the United States, and for other purposes."

Chapter Two

Why the United States Needed a Federal Reserve Act

I n 1913, banking in the United States had not changed since 1864, and people knew that the system needed to be updated. There had been a number of problems with the currency, or money, in use. Such problems often created crises, even though the country's economy was strong. With problem after problem, progressive-thinking Democrats and conservative Republicans decided it was time to work toward changing the banking system of the United States.

There were many people who had strong ideas about how to plan and change the United States' banking system. Now all that had to be decided was who would come up with the best plan and whose plan would gain enough support that it would pass in Congress.

At the time all this was taking place, Woodrow Wilson was the president of the United States. A strong personality, President Wilson thought he had the right and the

Small banks served particular communities. This photo shows the National German American Bank of St. Paul, Minnesota, circa 1870. Independent banks such as this one worked with a community to help people. The bank was not in business simply to make money.

responsibility to propose legislation and to help guide it through the legislative process. President Wilson was very busy with several different projects during his term as president. Nonetheless, he and his cabinet played a key role in constructing, altering, and passing the Federal Reserve Act of 1913.

President Wilson wanted to use the opportunity to set the banks and the country free from monopolies. Monopolies are companies that control a single business in a certain area. This allows the company to charge whatever prices it wants because there is no competition. Banking and currency reform became Wilson's top priority. It was true that bankers all over the country were unhappy with the way the banking system was being run. In the first two months of 1913, businessmen, manufacturers, bankers, and merchants wrote thousands of letters to Congress detailing just how bad the nation's current bank-

President Woodrow Wilson worked out a plan for the federal government to take control of the nation's banking system and money supply.

ing and currency systems were. They begged the House committee, led by Carter Glass, to take control and lead a reform of the system. And so a plan was put into place.

The plan was just what bankers needed. Unfortunately, it did not gain enough support in Congress. The plan was basically put on hold. One of the problems was that the Democrats were against giving bankers control of the Federal Reserve. They believed that federal officials should maintain control. President Wilson took charge and met

Saving the Banking System

A historian named Arthur Link wrote this summary of the 1911–19 Republican plan:

Senator Nelson W. Aldrich proposed a plan to solve the banking dilemma; this was supported by the American Bankers' Association. It provided for one great central bank, the National Reserve Association, with a capital of at least $100 million and with fifteen branches in various sections. The branches were to be controlled by the member banks on a basis of their capitalization. The National Reserve Association would issue currency, based on gold and commercial paper, that would be the liability of the bank and not of the government. It would also carry a portion of member banks' reserves, determine discount reserves, buy and sell on the open market, and hold the deposits of the federal government. The branches and businessmen of each of the fifteen districts would elect thirty out of the thirty-nine members of the board of directors of the National Reserve Association.

with experts and members of his party. Together they worked out the details and came to an agreement on the new banking and currency bill. Carter Glass, Dr. H. Parker Willis, and William McAdoo worked on the bill in secret. They had the support of bankers in Chicago, New York, and St. Louis. However, they also had some opposition. The Progressive wing of the Democratic Party was against the plan.

Democrats Carter Glass *(left)* and William Gibbs McAdoo *(right)* were powerful voices for change in America's banking system. They knew the country could only grow as strong as the bankers would let it, unless the government took control of the money supply. The deal Glass and McAdoo helped work out to form the Federal Reserve Act helped America become a financially secure country.

President Wilson and Carter Glass finally figured out a system that put the United States government in charge of the reserve system. The system also declared that the United States government was to issue the currency that would be used across the country.

15

Chapter Three

The Federal Reserve System

Although there were still some parties against President Wilson's bill, Wilson went forward with his plan. Finally, the president and his supporters were able to overcome the opposition as well as the various delays. On December 19, 1913, the Senate passed the Federal Reserve Bill, with a vote of 54–34 and with full support of the Democratic Party. President Wilson signed the Federal Reserve Bill on December 23, 1913.

Woodrow Wilson was re-elected president of the United States in 1916. Some historians mark the following year, 1917, as the end of the Progressive movement. That was the year the United States entered World War I. The Progressive movement was almost twenty years old by then, and it had done a great deal to improve conditions in the United States. Its main idea—that the government should and could act to resolve difficult economic and

America's involvement in the Progressive movement slowed when the country entered World War I in 1917. Troops went overseas on ships to help Europe end its bloody war. At home, the people wanted the country to be more stable. Progressives shook things up in politics and government. The people were ready to leave Progressive programs behind.

social issues—had worked well. Most Americans were happy with the results of the Progressive movement. The economy of the country truly was running more smoothly. However, things were not all smooth sailing for the rest of the century. More changes were ahead.

A Law That Changed History

Years after the Federal Reserve Act became official, in February 1924, strong words were written in the *New York Times* about the act: "It has been the habit of our people to speak of the enactment of the Federal Reserve law in December, 1913, as a piece of good luck for the country. 'Luck' it certainly was, when considered in the light of the possibility that without it the United States might have been swept along with Europe into depreciated paper money."

The months between October 1929 and December 1933 were a dismal period known in American history as the Great Depression. The stock market crashed, and many businesses failed right along with it. Many people lost their jobs and all their money. During the Great Depression, 1,300 banks collapsed. The Federal Reserve System was not prepared to prevent such collapse from happening, nor was it able to deal with the disaster.

As a consequence of the Great Depression, in 1933 the new Glass-Steagall Act required all the banks in the Federal Reserve System, which now numbered twelve, to insure their deposits. It also granted them greater authority to regulate credit and loans to customers. By doing this, the Federal Reserve would be better able to prevent its banks

During the Great Depression, banks closed when their money supply ran out. This left people penniless. They had no way of getting their money back. The Glass-Steagall Act, a part of the Banking Act of 1933, created the Federal Deposit Insurance Corporation (FDIC). The FDIC helped give local banks credit to insure people's savings in the bank. This move helped pull the country out of the Great Depression and kept the banking system stable.

from failing. Congress passed the act. This allowed the Federal Reserve to expand credit to its banks and also to make more of the federal gold supply available to businesses.

So, overall, what did the Federal Reserve Act do, officially? Several things. Most important, it made way for the

The stock market crash of 1929 cost millions of people all their money. Here, a Wall Street investor puts his car up for sale to earn some money on which to live.

Federal Reserve banks to be established. Then it created a currency that could change with the changing business of the country. Federal Reserve banks issued a new uniform currency that looked the same. The new paper money was called Federal Reserve notes. Eventually, these notes made up about 90 percent of the nation's currency in circulation. They would pass into circulation when member banks took loans from the Federal Reserve banks.

The Federal Reserve Act also made it easier to supervise the U.S. banking system. The Federal Reserve was similar to a parent bank, with each of the branches being its children. The parent bank set the rules on loans and rates of interest charges on those loans. It then checked in on each of its "children" to be sure they were following the rules correctly. Unofficially, it updated the banking system for the United States as well. The new system worked well across the many different levels of business needs. And more important, the system was equal and fair for businesses and citizens alike.

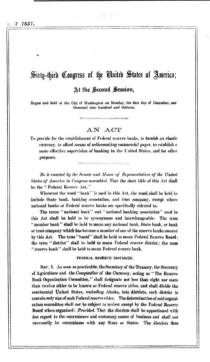

The Federal Reserve Act made law the reformation of America's banking system and money supply. Its effect has helped America have one of the most stable banking systems in the world.

The Banks of the Federal Reserve System

The Federal Reserve System is an independent central bank serving the United States of America. It divides the United States into twelve districts. Each district has its own bank as well as its own board of directors. Each board of directors makes its own policies and is responsible for preventing panics and bank failures.

The president of the United States appoints the chairman of the Federal Reserve System, known more commonly as the "Fed." This appointment has to be approved by the members of the United States Senate. However, the decisions made by the Federal Reserve System do not have to be ratified by the president or by anyone else in the executive or congressional branches of the United States government.

Each of the banks chartered under the National Banking Act of 1863 became members of the Federal Reserve System. Others were allowed to join, if they wished. The

This map of the United States shows how the Federal Reserve divided the country into twelve federal banking districts. Each district oversees state and local banks within its borders. The federal board works with the districts to set rates, give credit, and control the money supply.

president of the United States appoints a board of directors in Washington, D.C., to supervise and oversee the system.

Each district's main bank is responsible for the banks within a specific area. The First District, the Federal Reserve Bank of Boston, serves the six states of New England: Connecticut, New Hampshire, Maine, Massachusetts, Rhode

The Federal Reserve Banks

Broken up by districts (such as the First District, Second District, and so on), the twelve banks in the Federal Reserve are the Federal Reserve Bank of Boston, the Federal Reserve Bank of New York, the Federal Reserve Bank of Philadelphia, the Federal Reserve Bank of Cleveland, the Federal Reserve Bank of Richmond (Virginia), the Federal Reserve Bank of Atlanta, the Federal Reserve Bank of Chicago, the Federal Reserve Bank of St. Louis (Missouri), the Federal Reserve Bank of Minneapolis, the Federal Reserve Bank of Kansas City (Missouri), the Federal Reserve Bank of Dallas, and the Federal Reserve Bank of San Francisco.

Island, and Vermont. Organized in October 1914, the Federal Reserve Bank of Boston officially opened its doors for business on November 16, 1914. Located temporarily at the corner of Milk and Pearl Streets, the First District's bank had a staff of just three officers and fourteen clerks. By January 1, 1915, the Federal Reserve Bank of Boston had relocated to its new home at 53 State Street, a building that had once been home to the First National Bank of Boston. Within a short time, however, this space became too small and a larger, more conveniently located home for the bank was needed. For $1,400,000, the bank purchased

The first Federal Reserve Board in 1914 included *(seated, from left to right)* Charles S. Hamlin, W. G. McAdoo, F. A. Delano, *(standing, from left to right)* Paul M. Warburg, John Skelton Williams, W. P. G. Harding, and Adolf C. Miller. These men began the difficult task of taking control of the nation's money supply to regain the confidence of the American people in its system of government.

the premises at 95 Milk Street, with adjacent Pearl Street property, giving it a broad space that overlooked Boston's Pearl, Franklin, and Oliver Streets. Construction for the bank began in 1920. The large building was finished by 1922.

The Second District's bank is the Federal Reserve Bank of New York. It is located in New York City. The bank has a gold vault 100 feet (30 meters) below street level. Its depository is the largest in the world. Gold housed in the New York City bank belongs to several foreign nations,

Gold is no longer attached to the value of money in America. Its supply is still a standard of national wealth in case of financial disaster. Gold prices rise or fall depending on the gold supply and what people are willing to pay for it.

including Kuwait and Saudi Arabia, and is estimated to be valued at $25 billion!

The Seventh District bank is the Federal Reserve Bank of Chicago. The Seventh District serves a region of great economic diversity, including most of Illinois, Indiana, Michigan, Wisconsin, and all of Iowa. Although its head office is in Chicago, there is a branch office in Detroit, Michigan, and regional offices in Des Moines, Iowa; Indianapolis, Indiana; and Milwaukee, Wisconsin.

The Federal Reserve Bank of Chicago is responsible for several important things. It helps make national policies about money, it supervises and regulates banks and bank holding companies, and it provides financial services, such as check clearing and electronic payment processing, to banks and the United States government.

Many things have changed since the era during which the Federal Reserve Act came about to straighten out the American banking system. But one thing that has not changed is that today's banks are still running quite well under the Federal Reserve Act, and uniform currency is still being used across the country. It looks like President Wilson and his administration did good work for their people, not only at the time but for the future as well.

Glossary

corruption (kuh-RUP-shun) A lack of honesty.

crusaders (kroo-SAY-derz) Persons who take part in a campaign to get things changed for the better.

diversity (dih-VER-sih-tee) The condition or fact of being different.

domestic (duh-MES-tik) Of, relating to, made in, or done in one's own country.

economic (eh-kuh-NAH-mik) Of, relating to, or based on the making, selling, and using of goods and services.

immigrant (IH-muh-grint) A person who comes to a country to live there.

initiative (ih-NIH-shuh-tiv) A first step or movement.

journalist (JER-nuhl-ist) An editor or reporter of the news.

legislation (leh-jihs-LAY-shun) The action of making a law; the laws that are made.

medicinal (meh-DIS-in-ul) Used to relieve or cure disease.

monopoly (muh-NAH-puh-lee) A business owned by one group so it can control prices.

politician (pah-lih-TIH-shun) A person who is active in party politics or in conducting government business.

ratify (RA-tih-fy) To give legal approval to (as by vote).

recall (REE-koll) To cancel (as a law).

referendum (re-fuh-REN-dum) The idea or practice of letting the voters approve or disapprove laws.

reform (rih-FORM) To make better or improve by removal of faults; to improve what is bad.

sacramental (sak-ruh-MENT-uhl) Of or relating to a religious act or ceremony that is considered especially sacred.

social (SOH-shul) Of or relating to human beings as a group.

suffrage (SUH-frij) The right to vote.

welfare (WEL-fayr) Aid in the form of money or necessities for people who are poor, aged, or disabled.

Web Sites

Due to the changing nature of Internet links, the Rosen Publishing Group, Inc., has developed an online list of Web sites related to the subject of this book. This site is updated regularly. Please use this link to access the list:

http://www.rosenlinks.com/pmnhnt/fera

Primary Source Image List

Page 5: Cartoon illustration of J. P. Morgan controlling the New York City banks, appearing in *Puck*, circa 1910. Currently housed at the Library of Congress, Washington, D.C.

Page 7: Photograph of the Lakeland, Minnesota, town board meeting, 1898. Currently housed at the Minnesota Historical Society, St. Paul.

Page 9: Photograph of the National Progressive Convention held in Chicago, August 6, 1912. Currently housed at the Library of Congress, Washington, D.C.

Page 12: Photograph of the National German American Bank, St. Paul, circa 1870. Currently housed at the Minnesota Historical Society, St. Paul.

Page 13: Photograph of President Woodrow Wilson, circa 1913. Currently housed at the Library of Congress, Washington, D.C.

Page 21: The Federal Reserve Banks Act, December 23, 1913. Currently housed at the National Archives, Washington, D.C.

Page 23: Map of the United States showing the twelve Federal Reserve districts, circa 1920, by Theodor Horydczak. Currently housed at the Library of Congress, Washington, D.C.

Index

About the Author

Melanie Ann Apel is a freelance writer who lives in Chicago, Illinois.